# Pearls of Wisdom

*For That Notorious First Year & Forever After*

## *— For Him —*

# Pearls of Wisdom

*For That Notorious First Year & Forever After*

## — *For Him* —

## Clara Hinton

**New Leaf Press**

First Edition
September 1994

ISBN: 0-89221-273-X

Unless noted otherwise, Bible Scripture is from the New American Standard Version. JBP denotes the J.B. Phillips translation, NCV denotes the New Century Version, and NIV denotes the New International Version.

*This book is dedicated with all of Mom's love to
Michelle and Eric, Mike and Ashley, Dave and Cynthia,
and all of my treasures who will one day go through that
"Notorious First Year."*

# Introduction

If marriage is such a wonderful thing, then why do so many give up early in the game and look for a way out? That first year seems to be an incredibly difficult one for most couples. We go into this union so in love, blind to everything and everyone about us. And then it happens. Problems begin creeping into the relationship, and we don't know what is wrong. The whole thing seems like one big failure. This can't be what married life is all about! Adjustments. Attitudes. Bills. Responsibilities. Moods. Sharing. Boredom. Homesickness. Feeling abandoned at times. Where is this wedded bliss?

I, like so many others, went through a very difficult first year of marriage with my husband. Many doors were slammed, buckets of tears were shed, and there were many days of hardly speaking. Trying. Failing. Trying again. Wanting things to be different, but not knowing quite what to do.

Some 24 years and 11 children later, married life has not only survived, but has even managed to flourish! But it has not been easy. There have been compromises, adjustments, and much forgiveness all along the way.

Something still amazes me, though. When problems crop up (yes, they still do!), many of them relate back in some way to the very problems we experienced during that "notorious first year." Not long ago, this really hit home. My husband had to work out of town for a day and didn't know when he would return home that evening. As always, I reminded him to call me when he knew what his schedule would be. I simply wanted to know when I might expect him. At five minutes after twelve midnight, I received a phone call.

"Honey, I've been in Philadelphia and have several hours of driving yet to do. I'll see you in the morning." I could feel the blood warming in my veins! After these many years of marriage, it was amazing to me that my husband could still innocently "forget" to call home. He just got busy, had several appointments, and forgot.

The outcome of that episode is this book. I believe with all of my heart that most of us get lazy very early on in our married relationship. On top of that, very few of us know how to properly communicate with our mate. We need constant reminders and guidelines to help us get back on track, and to stay on track, whether it's that "fickle first year" or that "flourishing fiftieth year."

This book is an outpouring of love and wisdom accumulated over many years of trial and error, laughter and tears, and learning and re-learning. These "pearls" are meant to stimulate, challenge, encourage, and motivate us in our married lives. It is my sincere prayer that these "pearls" will help every married couple arrive back at the point where they began — with a pure, innocent, blinding love for one another, but equipped with the wisdom to keep this union of love bound, forevermore.

Lovingly,
Clara Hinton

Just as a rose is tender and beautiful, so is your wife. Treat her as such.

*"Husbands, love your wives and be gentle with them"*
(Col. 3:19;NCV).

Place your wife at the top of your priorities, and let her know she's at the top.

*"An excellent wife is the crown of her husband"*
(Prov. 12:4).

# Don't think in terms of "mine;" rather think in terms of "ours."

*"When you do things, do not let selfishness or pride be your guide"* (Phil. 2:3;NCV).

# Save some time each day just to talk to your wife.

*"I was asleep, but my heart was awake. A voice! My beloved was knocking"* (Song of Sol. 5:2).

# Angry words are never easily forgotten.

*"An angry person causes trouble; a person with a quick temper sins a lot"* (Prov. 29:22;NCV)

# Your wife's wishes should take priority over all others.

*"It is good and pleasant when God's people live in peace"* (Ps. 133:1;NCV).

# Be patient.

*"Love is . . . . patient"* (1 Cor. 13:4).

# Be honest in your failures.
# Your wife will love you
# for your honesty.

*"An honest answer is as pleasing as a kiss on the lips"*
(Prov. 24:26;NCV).

# Do not be jealous.

*"Wrath is fierce and anger is a flood, but who can stand before jealousy?"* (Prov. 27:4).

# Tell your wife often that you are thankful for her.

*". . . Let her love always make you happy"*
(Prov. 5:19;NCV).

# Open the car door for your wife.

*"Submit to one another out of reverence for Christ"*
(Eph. 5:21;NIV).

# Expect to give
# more than you get.

*"It is more blessed to give than to receive"* (Acts 20:35).

# Listen with your heart
# as well as with your ears.

*"I hear these things and my body trembles"*
(Hab. 3:16;NCV).

# A small unexpected act of kindness means much more than a big gift given from guilt.

*"People who work for peace and a peaceful way plant a good crop of right living"* (James 3:18;NCV).

# Be neat and clean with yourself.

*"Put on nice clothes and make yourself look good"*
(Eccles. 9:8;NCV).

# Do not invite dinner guests home without first asking.

*"A man who flatters his neighbor is spreading a net for his steps"* (Prov. 29:5).

# Prepare one meal a week just for your wife.

*"Better is a dish of vegetables where love is, than a fattened ox and hatred with it"* (Prov. 15:17).

# Help with the cleanup of dishes without being asked.

*"Whatever your hand finds to do,*
*do it with all your might"* (Eccles. 9:10).

# Continue to treat your wife as though you were still dating.

*"Be happy with the wife you married when you were young. She gives you joy, as your fountain gives you water"* (Prov. 5:18;NCV).

# Hold hands during a movie.

*"My lover's left hand is under my head, and his right arm holds me tight"* (Song of Sol. 8:3).

# Never leave the house without kissing your wife goodbye.

*"Worry is a heavy load, but a kind word cheers you up"* (Prov. 12:25;NCV).

# Tell your wife where you can be reached when you are away.

*"Therefore, however you want people to treat you,
so treat them"* (Matt. 7:12).

# Never make
# financial decisions alone.

*"Get advice if you want your plans to work"*
(Prov. 20:18;NCV).

# Never put down
# your mother-in-law.

*"Those who are careful about what they say keep
themselves out of trouble"* (Prov. 21:23;NCV).

# Don't compare your wife's cooking to your mother's.

*"Do not judge, lest you be judged"*
(Matt. 7:1).

# Help with the house cleaning.

*"In all the work you are doing, work the best you can.*
*Work as if you were doing it for the Lord, not for people"*
(Col. 3:23;NCV).

# Be responsible.

*"He who tills his land will have plenty of food, but he who follows empty pursuits will have poverty in plenty"*
(Prov. 28:19).

# Hold your temper
# and your tongue.

*"Foolish people lose their tempers, but wise people control theirs"* (Prov. 29:11;NCV).

# Treat your wife with respect. She is not your slave.

*"Nevertheless let each individual among you also love his own wife even as himself"* (Eph. 5:33).

# Don't bring your buddies home to "hang out" every night.

*"Some friends may ruin you"* (Prov. 18:24;NCV).

Bring a surprise home once in a
while — a flower, card, nightie,
or some bubble bath.

*"Oil and perfume make the heart glad"* (Prov. 27:9).

# If possible, call home once during the day just to say "I love you."

*". . . Put on love, which is the perfect bond of unity"*
(Col. 3:14).

# Daydream together.

*"A good person can look forward to happiness"*
(Prov. 10:28).

# Never compare your wife to others.

*"I am my beloved's and my beloved is mine"*
(Song of Sol. 6:3).

# Remember why you married this young lady.

*"For this cause a man shall leave his father and mother*
*and shall cleave to his wife,*
*and they shall become one flesh"* (Gen. 2:24).

# Don't bring work problems home. Leave them at the work place.

*"Don't always think about what you will eat or what you will drink, and don't keep worrying"* (Luke 12:29;NCV).

# Have a sense of humor, but do not make light of real problems.

*"Rejoice with those who rejoice, and weep with those who weep"* (Rom. 12:15).

# Your immaturity is not funny when you are married.

*"When I was a child, I talked like a child, I thought like a child. When I became a man, I stopped those childish ways"* (1 Cor. 13:11;NCV).

# Don't share your wife's private feelings with others.

*"He who goes about as a talebearer reveals secrets, but he who is trustworthy conceals a matter"* (Prov. 11:13).

# Never bring up previous girlfriends.

*"But avoid worldly and empty chatter, for it will lead to further ungodliness"* (2 Tim. 2:23).

# Do not carry arguments forward into another day.

*"Do not let the sun go down on your anger"* (Eph. 4:26).

# Do not pout when you don't always get your own way.

*"Better is a dry morsel and quietness with it, than a house full of feasting with strife"* (Prov. 17:1).

# Learn to give of yourself. Buying a gift never replaces giving of your time.

*"A man will be satisfied with good by the fruit of his words, and the deeds of a man's hands will return to him"*
(Prov. 12:14).

# When you do something nice, do not expect favors in return.

*"Trust in the Lord, and do good"* (Ps. 37:3).

# Learn to share.

*"And do not neglect doing good and sharing; for with such sacrifices God is pleased"* (Heb. 13:16).

# Empty the garbage
# without being asked.

*"Do all things without grumbling or disputing"*
(Phil. 2:14).

# Greet your wife first — before the newspaper, television, or the mail.

*"It takes wisdom to have a good family, and it takes understanding to make it strong"* (Prov. 24:3;NCV).

# Never put your wife on hold. If she has an urgent problem, deal with it now.

*"Understanding is like a fountain which gives life to those who use it"* (Prov. 16:22;NCV).

# Compliment your wife to others.

*"Give her the reward she has earned; she should be praised in public for what she has done"*
(Prov. 31:31;NCV).

# Do not be selfish in bed. Patience and tenderness are words to remember.

*"So husbands ought to love their own wives as their own bodies. He who loves his own wife loves himself"*
(Eph. 5:28).

# Be a good listener.

*"He who gives an answer before he hears, it is folly and shame to him"* (Prov. 18:13).

When your wife is upset, go to her, hold her, and let her know you will work things out.

*"By helping each other with your troubles, you truly obey the law of Christ"* (Gal. 6:2;NCV).

# Communicate your feelings.
# Your wife is not a mind reader.

*"People's thoughts can be like a deep well, but someone
with understanding can find the wisdom there"*
(Prov. 20:5;NCV).

# Remember that your wife is more interesting than the evening news.

*"Husbands, in the same way be considerate as you live with your wives, and treat them with respect . . ."*
(1 Pet. 3:7;NIV).

# Draw a hot bubble bath
# for your wife.

*"Do not merely look out for your own personal interests,
but also for the interests of others"* (Phil. 2:4).

Learn to say **"I love you"** often.

*"I will be so pleased if you speak what is right"*
(Prov. 23:16;NCV).

# Remind your wife how special she alone is.

*"Her husband praises her, saying, 'There are many fine women, but you are better than all of them' "*
(Prov. 31:29;NCV).

# Read a good book together.

*"Whoever listens to what is taught will succeed"*
(Prov. 16:20;NCV).

# Talk to your wife.
# She loves to hear your voice.

*". . . When he spoke he took my breath away"*
(Song of Sol. 5:6;NCV).

# Use eye contact when talking to your wife.

*"You have made my heart beat faster with a single glance of your eyes"* (Song of Sol. 4:9).

Learn how to break your wife's bad mood. Do not become part of her moods.

*"A soothing tongue is a tree of life"* (Prov. 15:4).

Help your wife through homesickness. Many new wives miss their mothers terribly.

*"Have I not wept for the one whose life is hard?"*
(Job 30:25).

# Be gentle.

*". . . Malign no one, be uncontentious, gentle, showing
every consideration for all men"* (Titus 3:2).

# Take your wife on a romantic walk.

*"My lover spoke and said to me, 'Get up my darling; let's go away, my beautiful one' "* (Song of Sol. 2:10;NCV).

# Kiss like you did before you were married.

*"May he kiss me with the kisses of his mouth! For your love is better than wine"* (Song of Sol. 1:2).

# Remember — this is new for both of you. Make allowances.

*". . . I don't understand . . . the way a man and woman fall in love"* (Prov. 30:18-19;NCV).

# Remember special days.
# Mark these boldly on your
# own special calendar.

*"There is a time for everything, and everything on earth has its special season"* (Eccles. 3:1;NCV).

# Never go to bed angry. Forget your problems through the night.

*"An angry man stirs up strife, and a hot-tempered man abounds in transgression"* (Prov. 29:22).

# Write your wife a poem.

*"How beautiful and how delightful you are, my love, with all your charms!"* (Song of Sol. 7:6).

Plan a romantic evening of candlelight and soft music.

*"At night on my bed, I looked for the one I love"*
(Song of Sol. 3:1).

# Learn to compromise. Many problems take some giving on both parts.

*"With patience you can convince a ruler, and a gentle word can get through to the hard-headed"*
(Prov. 25:15;NCV).

# Never publicly embarrass your wife.

*"Those who are careful about what they say protect their lives, but whoever speaks without thinking will be ruined"* (Prov. 13:3;NCV).

# Touch often. A warm touch says more than a hundred words.

*"Furthermore, if two lie down together they keep warm, but how can one be warm alone?"* (Eccles. 4:11).

# Expect the best.

*"Now faith is being sure of what we hope for and certain of what we do not see"* (Heb. 11:1;NIV).

# Remember that hearts can be broken. Handle with care.

*"The spirit of a man can endure his sickness, but a broken spirit, who can bear?"* (Prov. 18:14).

When in doubt what to say or do,
follow your heart.

*"Let the words of my mouth and the meditation of my
heart be acceptable in Thy sight"* (Ps. 19:14).

# It takes a long time to erase a harsh word.

*"A brother offended is harder to be won than a strong city"* (Prov. 18:19).

# Make each day special in some way.

*"People ought to enjoy every day of their lives, no matter how long they live"* (Eccles. 11:8;NCV).

Love your wife's family. She will always be a part of them.

*"Make your father and mother happy; give your mother reason to be glad"* (Prov. 23:25;NCV).

# Watch a sunrise together.

*"Sunshine is sweet; it is good to see the light of day"*
(Eccles. 11:7;NCV).

# Give lots of hugs.

*". . . There is a time to hug"* (Eccles. 3:5;NCV)

# Give your wife some time to do girl things with her friends.

*"Do not withhold good from those to whom it is due, when it is in your power to do it"* (Prov. 3:27).

# Be your wife's best friend.

*"A friend loves at all times"* (Prov. 17:17).

# Be a responsible provider.

*"But if anyone does not provide for his own, and especially for those of his household, he has denied the faith, and is worse than an unbeliever"* (1 Tim. 5:8).

# Be a gentleman at all times.

*"There must be no evil talk among you, and you must not speak foolishly or tell evil jokes. These things are not right for you"* (Eph. 5:4;NCV).

# Time spent with your wife should be more important than time spent with your buddies.

*"And Jacob served seven years for Rachel; and they seemed unto him but a few days, for the love he had for her"* (Gen. 29:20).

# Choose a hobby that you both enjoy.

*"Two people are better than one, because they get more done by working together"* (Eccles. 4:9;NCV).

# Love your wife even when she is at her worst.

*"Love knows no limits to its endurance"*
(1 Cor. 13:7;JBP).

# Treat your wife as though she is a special gift.

*"An excellent wife, who can find? For her worth is far above jewels"* (Prov. 19:14).

# Love your wife into a good mood.

*"Husbands, love your wives, and do not be embittered against them"* (Col. 3:19).

Sleep in the bedroom, not in front of the television or when your wife is trying to talk to you.

*"If you love to sleep, you will be poor"*
(Prov. 20:13;NCV).

# When your wife makes absolutely no sense, love her anyway.

*"Enjoy life with the woman whom you love all of your fleeting life which He has given to you under the sun"* (Eccles. 9:9).

# Love your wife for who she is **right now.**

*"He who finds a wife finds a good thing and obtains favor from the Lord"* (Prov. 18:22).

# Remember that to your wife, tenderness is strength.

*"Put on a heart of compassion, kindness, humility, gentleness, and patience . . ."* (Col. 3:12;NAS).

# Express your feelings of love by your actions.

*"We should love not only with words and talk, but by our actions and true caring"* (1 John 3:18;NCV).

# Being stubborn is *not* a sign of being strong.

*"Whoever is stubborn after being corrected many times will suddenly be hurt beyond cure"* (Prov. 29:1;NCV).

# Always pull together on major issues.

*"May the God who gives endurance and encouragement give you a spirit of unity among yourselves as you follow Christ Jesus"* (Rom. 15:5;NIV).

# Don't remind your wife of your good points. She already knows them.

*"If you have been foolish in exalting yourself . . . put your hand on your mouth"* (Prov. 30:32;NAS).

# When you say you'll be home by seven, be home by seven.

*". . . Don't break your promises, but keep the promises you make"* (Matt. 5:33;NCV).

# All work and no play makes a husband a very distant person.

*"One handful of rest is better than two fists of labor striving after wind"* (Eccles. 4:6;NAS).

# Hold your wife closely at least once each day.

*"When a man takes a new wife, he shall . . . give happiness to his wife whom he has taken"* (Deut. 24:5).

# Back the words "I'm sorry" with actions that truly mean "I'm sorry."

*"Let love be without hypocrisy. Abhor that which is evil. Cling to what is good. . . . Do not let evil defeat you, but defeat evil by doing good"* (Rom. 12:9-21;NAS).

*These Pearls of Wisdom are sure to help you get through*
*the adjustments of that Notorious First Year together.*
*Build on these Pearls and in the years to come you are*
*sure to have a life of untold happiness together.*

*May God bless you to that end!*